HUMAN MIND, AWAKENING AND MANAGEMENT
Mystical Writings

HUMAN MIND, AWAKENING AND MANAGEMENT

Mystical Writings

Satish Kumar

KALPAZ PUBLICATIONS
DELHI–110 052

1. *The Part-1 of the book was published by the author himself in 2000 for limited circulation only, in the name of 'Let Us Search Ourselves'.*
2. *The views expressed in this book are entirely of the author and may or may not tally exactly with any of the scriptures. The author is not responsible for any misinterpretations drawn and their ill usage.*
3. *Stories given in the book may be treated as factitious.*

HUMAN MIND, AWAKENING AND MANAGEMENT
Mystical Writings
(Psychology, Philosophy)

Rs. 450

ISBN: 81-7835-109-9

Published in 2002 in India by
Kalpaz Publications
C-30, Satyawati Nagar
Ashok Vihar Phase-III
Delhi-110 052
E-mail: Kalpaz@hotmail.com

Lasertypesetting at: Varsha Graphics, Delhi
Printed at Chawla Offset Printers, Delhi 110 052

Contents

PART—2
Focus : Human Behaviour

A message ...

Happiness is dear to everyone. Everyone longs for it, waits for it and dreams for an everlasting happiness.

I ask many a question, "Are you 100 percent happy?" I rarely get the answer, "Yes". Then I ask, "Are you 80 percent happy ?" Some say, "Yes", whereas others say, even lesser. 80 percent happy means you are 20 percent anxious or sad. The question is, 20 percent of what? Our thoughts are a mixture of some good and bad feelings. The higher the percentage of good feelings, the higher is the happiness. It is, therefore, our thoughts that make us happy and it is our thoughts that make us sad. Generally, we first think and then act. Our actions, therefore, play a great role in making us happy, but all the same they are based on our thoughts.

Mind, the chunchal mun, is nothing but our thinking capacity. It is a mischievous element, an uncontrollable and unbridled horse. It is always on the run. Apart from joys and sorrows it brings in us envy, pride and anger, etc.

The key to happiness, therefore, lies within you. One can find happiness in what one has. A man may have a lot but less happiness and a man may have less but more happiness.

Will and determination, which take us to the pinnacle of success depend a lot on the state of one's mind, one's thoughts. In the following pages, I have placed my views, based on my experience and more so on the knowledge flow through meditation, which I have been practising for more than 35 years. When the mind gets fully absorbed in that immaculate part of the God, i.e., soul, one gets supreme happiness.

Satish Kumar

"He who is not a source of annoyance to his fellow-creatures, and who in his turn does not feel vexed with his fellow-creatures, and who is free from delight and envy, perturbation and fear, he is dear to ME."

Srimad Bhagavadgita
Ch.12

PART—1

Focus : Mind Management

The awakening

My body is a hut,
Who lives in that,
is a million dollar but,
My thoughts live in that,
My dreams live in that,
My anger lives in that,
My pride lives in that,
But again, there is a million dollar but,
Who controls all this rut,
It is I who control,
It is me who controls,
It is none else who controls,
Or is it HE who controls,
It is a questionable question, we, therefore,
put a cut to this but,
To ponder there is within you a shining
dazzling nut,
which illuminates and awakens the whole hut.

- *The nut is your soul within you and not your mind.*
- *The mind means thinking faculties whereas the soul is an immaculate part of the creator.*
- *The mind runs, runs and runs, which is a never ending process.*
- *The best exercise to control mind is meditation.*

Coexistence

The stars, the sun, the moon, the earth
and other planets
cannot exist alone,
The mouth, the nose, the hands, the legs
cannot live alone,
The existence of the man depends upon
the coexistence of
many a natural laws,
then how a man can live alone ?
The differences that occur
cannot occur alone,
Let us solve the differences as a
man cannot live alone,
Let us accept others as you and me
cannot live alone.

* *One dies alone, but one cannot exist alone.*

- *Before harbouring a grudge, try to be a good judge, as a good judge cannot be a judge with a grudge.*

- *There is nothing else besides ME. Like clusters of yarn beads formed by knots on a thread, all this is threaded on ME.*

Srimad Bhagavadgita
Ch.7

What's life

The morning sun that greets you,
The morning breeze that meets you,
It is like awakening that treats you,
There is something in this time that stimulates you.

The afternoon sun that heats you,
The sunny gloomy luck that cultivates you,
It is your experience with life that at times sweats you,
It is how you take, your life educates you.

Now, it is the twilight time that awaits you,
The cumbersome life at times irritates you,
A little enjoyment none the less activates you,
This is how the life agitates you.

The dark night sometimes worries you, at times motivates you,
The life slowly mitigates you,
A time comes the life repudiates you,
This is how the life grates you.

- *Life is a Journey full of zeal, pleasure and happiness, if you concentrate and get guided by the one who creates you.*

- *Confide with HIM, the creator.*

- *The more you reach near HIM, the more you enjoy life. This enjoyment is far more than the one achieved through worldly matters.*

The flight of a mind

It flies, flies and flies,
anybody, no concern.
It wants to enjoy, enjoy and enjoy,
anybody, no concern.
It is uncontrollable,
anybody, no concern.
It may crash,
anybody, no concern.
I will fly,
anybody, no concern.
Let me clash and crash,
anybody, no concern.
Is it unquestionable,
a little concern.
No, No, No questions,
Let it be anybody's concern.
I will not think further,
it's none of my concern.
I will catch up any thing,
it's my concern.
I will fly,
it's my concern.
But, it may tire me one day,
it's not my concern.

I may consider,
it's not my concern.
I have the power to fly,
it's my concern.
Who can question it,
may be anybody's concern.
Thinking and considering,
it's none of my concern.
What maturity,
it's none of my concern.
But one day I may have to consider and think,
it may be my concern.
But I want to fly,
it's my concern.
However, to think, consider, weigh, decide and fly
can be my concern.
Yes,
it may be a wise concern.

My mind is fugitive

My mind is never free,
It wanders without a licence or fee,
It can see what the eyes can't see,
It is at times with a she and at times with a he.
My mind is never free,
No one can chain it, it escapes scotfree,
Left to it, it becomes as selfish as a bee,
It creates jealousy and anger as huge as a rock tree.
My mind is never free,
It has one target, it wants to remain in glee,
Even if, I close my eyes, it tends to flee,
When chained to God, it is no more free,
it is with me.

- *I consider them to be the best yogis who endowed with supreme faith, and ever united through meditation with ME, worship ME with the mind centred on ME.*

Srimad Bhagavadgita
Ch.12

What do I give

I have little money to live,
I have a few things to live,
Let me search what do I give ?
I have just enough to live,
At times I have to borrow to live,
I take against anything I do, but what to give ?
But I think I have a stock of costfree things to give,
I have a stock of sweet words to give,
I have a stock of respectful words to give,
I have a stock of some wisdom to give,
I have a stock of some love to give,
I have a stock of some sincere love to give.

* *Keep anything in the stock of your thoughts but not hatred and revenge.*

What I possess

What I have in my bag,
Some papers, some clothes and metals all the same,
I feel, I am playing only a game.
Of course, I have put my tag on my bag,
I have a beautiful, self styled name,
All the same, it is a part of my game.
What else is in my bag ?
Let me search, have a dig,
I may find something big.
There is nothing big in my bag,
Bigger than big is HIS name,
If it is not a part of my game.
It is only HIS name which makes my bag a bag,
Otherwise it is only a rag.

Patience

At times when I am nearing the near,
The gap becomes difficult to bear,
In the mind of my minds, it is all clear,
But it seems that the near is no more near.
The goal becomes all the more dear,
I want to steer at the top gear,
But there is something that stops me steer,
I start losing faith in HIM, whom I am so near.
I feel the morning will be clear,
Will it be foggy, it is only a fear,
I will never forget HIM, I swear,
Let me reach, this time that near.
Will I survive to that truth, is also not clear,
My impatience, at times, makes me tear,
I get nervous, I can't bear,
God alone help me to soothe my mind till I reach that near.

- *Train your mind, Patience is not so easy to achieve.*
- *Impatient minds dash and crash, whereas patient minds remain calm even in difficult times.*
- *Patience is the best medicine for stress, worries and anger.*
- *A patient has to remain patient till the time he recovers.*

That splendid view

What did I do, let me review,
I was busy with something, nothing new,
I got whatever was due.
Some wishes still remained is a matter to view,
One wish dies and the other springs up, its not new,
If I will remain dancing to the wishes of my mind,
can anyone give a clue.
Thinking and doing, seconds, minutes, hours,
months and years just flew,
Thoughts, thoughts and thoughts, it was a big queue,
Some struck like glue, others went off like morning dew.
Certain moments are, however, always new,
These moments have a different hue,
When I have HIS splendid view.

Unjustified hunger

Is my demand from me just ?
Is my demand from others just ?
Is others demand from me just ?
An emotional just does not see what is just.

I must get that and that is a must,
A bigger car is a must,
A bigger building is a must,
A blind lust does not see what is just.

Let me develop a considerate must,
Let me envelop myself into a well thought of must,
Let me not bring must to the brim of the must,
I may amend what I call just.

Emotions

A signal flashes,
Sometimes my anger flashes,
Sometimes my ego flashes,
There is something within me that clashes.

I feel as if someone lashes,
Sometimes my pride lashes,
Sometimes my lust lashes,
There is something within me that clashes.

Against me, there is something that crashes,
My body crashes, my lumbar crashes,
All the same everything dashes and crashes,
When I again remember that I am all ashes.

Transcending

Have I gone astray ?
I have to analyse,
Make myself wise.
Let me think if I have gone astray ?
Do I need an advice,
Self evaluation can be a good device.
I hope I can find the right way if I have gone astray ?
I have to search my conscience justly,
To take a self disciplined decision correctly.
I shall find in anyway if I have gone astray ?
I may not get biased,
I have to remain unbiased.
I feel I require a ray of sunshine to find if I have gone astray ?

Finding faults is easy

Who is afraid of criticism ?
How foolish the way he walks,
How awkward he talks.
Let me see if it is a biased criticism ?
But, who is perfect ?
Everyone suffers from one or the other defect.
Then, what criticism ?
It makes me fight,
At times, I have restless night.
But, what benefit one gets from criticism ?
It makes me aware of my weakness,
A healthy criticism also shows nearness.
Let me build strength within to face criticism,
Let me show a biased criticism a logical low hoot,
If unbiased, let me reach it's root.
In anyway, I shall win over criticism.

The thinking time

This is the right time for thinking,
Not thinking over the sadness,
But, thinking the causes of sadness.
Let me develop a positive thinking,
By thinking let me not get into sadness,
By thinking let me get over the sadness.
Let me train my mind to do the right thinking,
Let me not develop or plan anyone's sadness,
Let me not develop or plan the removal of other's happiness.
Let me think about the right way of thinking,
Let me not convert anyone's happiness into sadness,
Let me convert anyone's sadness into happiness.
Let me not develop a habit of negative thinking.

God made everyone equal

It is man only who made the name,
Otherwise, for HIM everyone is the same.
Someone calls that man a good man,
The other one calls the same man a bad man.
Someone adores that man,
The other one hates that man.
But, the God has made that man only a man,
It is the man who labelled that man.
What is different man to man?
Of course, the appearances are different.
More particularly, the thoughts are different.
It is mainly the thoughts within a man that make
him different.
It is the thinking sight that makes two men different.
Or is it, the God who made two men different.

Troublesome bubble

I know that I am a bubble,
I know I create for my own sake unnecessary trouble.
Actually, I forget that I am a bubble,
I know, my ever flying mind creates all this trouble.
It makes me fly and fly like a soap bubble,
Up and down, allowed I create trouble.
Had I been soft like a soap bubble,
I would not have put others to trouble.
At that time I forget that I am a bubble,
Actually, forgetting what I am is my trouble.
I remember, I again realise that I am a bubble,
When I see a bubble crash or a bubble in trouble.
If I remember, only sometimes, that I am a bubble,
Atleast, I would not put others to trouble.

* *Bubble + Trouble = Rubble.*

TIME : The all time player

The clock is ticking,
The heart is throbbing,
The time is slipping,
Am I slipping or the time is slipping ?

The trees are budding,
The newly borns are crying,
The young one's are singing,
Time is not slipping, it is I who is slipping.

The life passes laughing and crying,
The life sees many slipping,
The time is only watching,
I think I am slipping.

The life is gripping,
The life is dodging,
The life is dying,
The all time player, the great TIME is always watching.

* *TIME, the all time player watches and records everything. Therefore, build an image that the world remembers you after you.*

God and I

I am Hard, HE is Soft,
I am Weak, HE is Strong,
I am Restless, HE is Patient,
I am Angered, HE is Polite,
I am Revengeful, HE is Forgiving,
I am a Player, HE is an Organiser,
I am Biased, HE is Unbiased,
I am at times Unjust, HE is always Just,
I see only the Present, HE sees the Past, Present & Future,
I am, therefore, Unwise, HE is all Wise.

'THE CRUX'

The fruits HE provides us are enormous, some are bitter, some are sour and some sweet. But fruit is a fruit, one at times enjoys bitterness also.

Is anger equal to mild madness

Anger is a blaze within a man.
It can burn you,
Don't let it govern you.
Anger is a disease within a man.
Don't let it beat you,
Control it or you do not know how it will treat you.
Anger is a weakness within a man.
Don't let it defeat you,
Don't let it retreat you.
Anger can be a power within a man.
If one uses it sparingly,
If one uses it mildly and Wisely.
Anger is indeed a fire within a man.

* *A proper governance of the mind machine can cure anger.*

In the web of thoughts

Thoughts invade me,
Thoughts irritate me,
Thoughts calm me,
Thoughts degrade me,
Thoughts elevate me,
Thoughts weaken me,
Thoughts strenghten me,
Thoughts harden me,
Thoughts soften me,
Thoughts dictate me,
Thoughts educate me,
Thoughts silently invade me.

'THE CRUX'

Day in, day out, thoughts silently and stealthily invade and conquer the doer who bears the fruits of good and bad.

The pride in me

I am all superior,
I have a better job,
I have a better bungalow,
I have a better car,
I have a better status.
But, on turning around, I find myself inferior;
He has a better job,
He has a better income,
He has a better property,
He has a better image.
Who is to judge if I am superior or inferior ?
How to determine the superiority or inferiority ?
Is it wealth that determines the superiority ?
Is it the job that determines the superiority ?
Or is it the status that determines the superiority ?
I feel it is the values of life that determine the superiority,
I feel it is the wiseness within a man that determines
the superiority,
I feel, the wiser one is, the lesser is the difference between
inferiority and superiority,
I think, it is the sanity that determines one's superiority.

- *The excessive pride in a person is a disease which erodes him from within.*
- *A tidy and stable mind alone can win over pride.*

Is it beyond my reach

It was a happy time,
It was a loving time,
It was a wonderful time,
It was a gaining time.
Is it possible to control the changing colours of time ?
It is a terrible time,
It is a devastating time,
It is a parting time,
It is a crying time.
Is it beyond my reach to change the changing time ?
But, it is a testing time,
It is an adjusting time,
It is an adapting time,
It is a learning time.
Yes, it is within my reach to change myself according to the
changing time.

* *Past is buried in the past. Present is to take action and adapt oneself to the changing seasons of time.*

It is never too late to reform

My temperament is mine,
I am not a divine,
He has to fall in my line.
My temperament is mine,
I am a leonine,
He will be made to align.
My temperament is mine,
A little adjustment, as if I have to pay fine,
But, a little adjustment, others may feel fine.
Still, my temperament is mine,
Of course, I am not a divine,
Adaptation can however, be a way to align.
I do understand my temperament is not that fine.

Measure of success

What is success ?
For some to be a clerk is success,
For others to be an officer is success,
For another to be an IAS is success.
What is the measure of success ?
Is it the money that matters ?
Or is it the status that matters ?
Or is it a particular post that matters ?
Who has made this measure of success ?
Is it the God who has made it ?
Or is it the society who has made it ?
Or is it my own mind who has made it ?
Yes, it is my own mind who has made this
measure of success.

- *Success is measured by the units of desire, need and greed in one's mind.*

- *Happiness and success are the by-products of one's thoughts and deeds alone.*

- *We set one goal, try to achieve it, set another goal and so on. Sometimes we get less and sometimes in excess. Success or failure it is only a guess. One's mind gets busy to assess. But to facilitate, one needs His access.*

Man is great

Fate is Fate,
The man is still great.
Can a man create fate ?
What can a man create ?
The Sun, I can't create,
The Moon, I can't create,
The Earth, I can't create.
The man can, of course, use the raw materials of the God's wonderful estate,
The man can erect high structures on God's estate,
The man can eat tasty eatables of the God's estate,
The man can put a name tag on a piece of God's estate.
But, can a man create fate ?
He can find ways to fight fate,
A man can indeed fight fate,
A man can wage a war against fate,
But, can he create fate ?

Speech

Let me control my speech,
Why, it has the freedom,
It's my kingdom.
Who can put a curb on my speech ?
Afterall, what does it cost ?
But, does the words get lost ?
Words hurt a lot, let me think of a soft speech,
Let me not use words in haste,
Words are precious, meaningful and not waste.
Let me think of a polite speech,
I can yell, of course, I can yell,
But, it may make someone's life a hell.
Let me think of a more mature speech.

A bouquet or a flower

You may present a flower,
Or you may present a tower,
It is a token of sincere feelings,
How much sincere depends upon your dealings.

A gift is a gift,
It may soothe one's feelings,
Good and wise words are also a gift,
May we use good words to soothe one's feelings.

Your dealings may not be a true reflection of your feelings,
A gift may not be a true reflection of your feelings,
Let us not abuse the flowers as a reflection of our feelings,
Let us present the flowers after having sincere, true and flowery feelings.

When sorrows descend

I do not know when it creeps in me,
I cannot know when it surrounds me,
I only come to know when it completely saddens me,
A time later, I feel something has hardened me.

I get vexed,
I no more feel relaxed,
I get fazed and completely dazed,
My mind gets completely hazed.

I do not like anyone, nor does anyone like me in that state,
Almost everything I just hate,
Good and Joyous thoughts hesitate,
Fun and Jokes irritate.

I think of, if anyone can guide and teach me,
I think of, if anyone who can help me,
I think of only God in meditation who can heal me,
It is finally the God who helps, teaches me and retrieves me.

Pleasure is mine

I want to remain always in pleasure,
What have I to do to get pleasure,
Have I to attain a lot of wealth to get pleasure,
Have I to do special jobs to get pleasure,
I want to live always in pleasure,
Is there a cost I have to pay for pleasure,
Let me know who distributes pleasure,
Is it friends or relatives that can give me pleasure,
I want to rejoice always in pleasure,
Who holds the key to the pleasure,
I want to reach the treasure of pleasure,
Where should I dig to generate pleasure,
I think, it is I and not others who hold the key to my pleasure.

- *Mind is a pivot balancing the joys and sorrows in one's life.*

The will that matters

It is the will that makes you feel weak,
It is the will that makes you feel strong,
It is the will that generates energy in you,
It is the will that accelerates your pace in life,
It is the will that makes you honest,
It is the will that makes you corrupt.
Let us use our will in the positive direction,
Let us not use our will to lose our destination,
Let us use our will in the positive generation,
Let us not use our will for degeneration,
Let us use our will for a successful culmination,
Let us not use our will for man's retardation.

- *Mind Power = Will Power*
- *Mind power is the genesis of will and determination which take us to the pinnacle of success.*

The give and take mechanism

Took	*Gave*
1. Body	
2. Food	
3. Air	
4. Water	?
5. Earth	
6. Atmosphere	
7. Money	
8. Shelter	
9. Love	
10. Happiness	
And What Not	

? *From the God's Estate you have taken everything. But, what have you given ?*

Check out you may not get into a debt trap.

- *The greatest temple on the earth is your own body where inhabits the Almighty in reality.*

What for I am here

What is my goal ?
What is my role ?
Why have I come on this earth ?
Why have I taken birth ?

Yes, I have to look after my life,
I have to pay attention to my wife,
I feel at times, I have no role,
Everything is under HIS control.

Why, I have to look after my child,
He may, otherwise, go wild,
My child will become as I train,
I feel again, this falls under HIS domain.

Then, what have I to look for?
Then, what have I to live for ?
Is my role to go gay, eat and sleep,
Or have a big illusory leap.

Is my role to make abundant money,
And enjoy, make glee and eat honey,
But, this is also under the surveillance of that magnanimous designer,
That is also the creation of the divine choreographer.

I think, I now can envisage my goal,
My inner vision is directing me this role,
Perhaps, when my mind merges with the immaculate soul,
That may be my ultimate goal.

- *As the one Sun illuminates this entire universe, so the one Atma (Spirit) illuminates the whole Kshetra (body).*

Srimad Bhagavadgita
Ch. 13

We are all the beads of the same yarn threaded together through our souls to the Almighty, sharing the same atmosphere and same surface. Pushing or shoving someone will naturally have an equal and opposite effect, if not this moment, some other moment.

—Author

PART—2

Focus : Human Behaviour

The beauty of nature

The sun that appears and disappears regulated over the year,
Unfolds the beauty of the earth wide and clear,
The fresh air that comes with it caressing its ray,
Tells us to sit in the lap of nature and start a fresh day.

The light brings everywhere a delight,
With new hopes and colours to everyone's sight,
It is God's light that falls on the earth,
That is why it can enter every corner without dearth.

The nature provides us all the things,
And carries with it, with love in its wings,
The nature reminds us of an unceasing action,
And we being nature's part, expects from us a similar reaction.

The nature's actions are mostly steady and slow,
The fast one's come generally with a devastating blow,
The God's nature is present everywhere to teach,
A deluded mind thinks, it is beyond its reach.

The nature endlessly sings a song of love and no vice,
A sinful mind unaware of HIM keeps an eye only on his dice,
A sincere and willing eye on HIM can break all ice,
Have patience, the nature will provide you its palatable slice.

- *You are part of the nature, the nature is within and surrounding. There is no escape from learning and knowing HIM.*
- *The nature in its beauty reveals many guiding secrets.*

I am the source of all creation and everything in the world moves because of ME; knowing thus the wise, full of devotion, constantly worship ME.

Srimad Bhagavadgita
Ch.10

Emotionally mature

Do I stir others feelings unnecessarily ?
Do my feelings get disturbed so easily ?
Balanced feelings make a man stable,
A man with unstable feelings, is rudely called,
'The Unable'.

How to manage a feeling ?
From where to bring in healing ?
To a physically strong man, can the feelings give a blow ?
Masculine physique, minus feelings make a man rather low.

Feelings make a big show,
Sometimes tears and sometimes smiles, I don't know,
The one who can manage the feelings, steals the show,
Feelings can play such a role that even after defeat,
you may glow.

Day in, day out, eating, singing, walking and talking,
One never knows, when the feelings start stirring if
not rocking,
The intelligent one's can see the stirring on one's face,
Even without talking it changes one's gaze.

Sometimes, one wants to disturb someone intentionally,
The result of this mischief comes out instantly,
If the subject is strong at its root,
He will not care the mischief maker and won't hoot.

Stirring of emotions can do vast harm,
It can blow houses and humans without alarm,
Wise one's, therefore, try not let others and their own emotions go out of control,
They envisage their own action and others reactions and as such fix accordingly their own role.

- *Emotions play a great role, master them or get mastered, leading to burns of jealousy and anger.*
- *Removal of thoughts stirring the emotions and getting involved in other interesting jobs can be of great help.*
- *Meditation is undoubtedly of great help.*

The unexpected happenings

Always does not happen the expected,
The rhyme of life is not always as predicted,
The seeker is mostly dejected,
Arises a storm of feelings leaving agitated.

The man curses himself, others and the God,
It is luck only, there is no one to guard,
Everyone gets each and everything,
It is I who is gifted with none and nothing.

Amid agony ends a bitter story,
Without faith in himself and others, the life lacks glory,
Frustration may either make the life still slow,
Or a ripe thinking may make the life go.

Understanding the reality is one way,
The sun does not shine in every part of the world all day,
The nature nourishes every living being as per its share,
With one's wrong past deeds, one may lose his
share somewhere.

It is possible, what one thinks is the right ending,
Is not possibly for you, wait for the right bending,
Life sees happenings good and bad mixed,
Let us have faith in nature, and let's not get miffed.

- *Before taking an invading action against someone, think its righteousness. You may not get a backlash from the nature.*

- *A man is a part of nature. Nature in its wings carries devastating weapons also.*

The stubborn one's

Let me admit, when a mistake I commit, who stops,
Let's see confession or my conceit, who tops,
A conceited mind can't admit so easily,
Humility overpowering an adamant mind, very rarely.

A stubborn is a difficult thing to control,
A human being so brittle as a whole,
The tone of voice brittle, even the laugh brittle,
The sufferings and others feelings, feels very little.

Runs off from the word persuasion,
Adjustment, he is far off from simple cooperation,
Perhaps, he shuts his doors to that inward noise,
Perhaps, he is far off from what is called poise.

Why can't a person be adjusting and cooperating in nature?
Even when it is some good animals gesture,
Only his thinking capabilities can make him wise,
A logical thought, reasoning and intellect can make him rise.

Let him see the growth of a tree and its fruits, how nature works in unison,
Let him see his own body, how each part works in unison,
Only if he agrees to open the gates of his mind,
A nicer, peaceful and beautiful world is waiting behind.

- *The best way for a stubborn to reform is to just start listening to others, think of others views and talk less.*
- *A search within can make a stubborn realize others feelings and sufferings.*

Caring relationships

Spoken in haste or otherwise, matters a single word,
It may catch up fire or melt someone when heard,
The fire, at times, is so intense, it gets out of control,
The speaker thinks, where I went wrong in my role.

Not only words, the pitch of the voice also matters,
I may speak louder and louder what deters,
If I have to see harmony around me,
Then, I should not depend on the action of you, she or he.

First, let me be concerned about what I do,
Next comes the role of he, she or who,
First, let me control my own action,
Then, I may think of controlling others reaction.

Have I the right to say nasty words, if someone does wrong?
No, till I have invested in others feelings care and love earlier, not that long,
The feelings of the others have to be harnessed at the right hours,
Sincere words, love and small gifts, it does not require towers.

How to maintain nice and heart loving relations?
How to have wonderful and meaningful connections?
Logical words, understanding each other can have nice endings,
Soft and control on words can see many harsh beings weddings.

- *Relationships develop not with arrogance but with sweetness.*
- *If one feels harshness has done some good to him, that good may not be momentary.*

Win or lose, it's life

One who gets a prize is wise,
One who does not get it, is not that wise,
You have lost only in one field,
Keep on racing, never yield.

One has won one race,
You may win another, only if ready to face,
What insult or disgrace,
Life is a never ending race.

All battles are fought to be won,
But, a battle can be won only by one,
Fighting a battle is man's duty,
The rest is all nature's beauty.

Battles are fought outside,
And battles are fought within,
You may win a battle outside,
Still the win is not a win if you lose the battle within.

You may lose a game outside,
But, you have not lost till you don't lose within,
Outside and inside battles are not alike,
Even, solution to certain battles may lie within.

You may lose, learn again and be wise,
The defeat will make you analyse,
Confidently shake hands with your defeat,
If you have decided not to retreat.

- *A losing person will always look back his steps, as to where he went wrong.*
- *An analysis of your weaknesses may help you turn them into strengths.*
- *Tears have no place in life. Think and be strong.*

The hunger for money

The money hunger is different from hunger for food,
The latter subsides after eating, the former increases after getting,
The hungry stomach asks for food after getting empty,
after sometime,
The money stuck hearts long for it, even after huge netting.

It is the nature built network of senses, that creates hunger of different tastes,
The blurred mind is caught in the web of its own hungry designs,
Whatever be the outcome, the mind remains undisturbed,
It is the being who wears ultimately the thirsty signs.

The man worships God to provide him huge money,
If the prayers are sincere, the God may fill his bags with honey,
Will it satisfy him and his thirst?
Will his overall situation be better with more money or get worst?

It is a big question, which the man does not know,
For more money he again takes a go,
Whether more money can bring him pleasure,
Or, is it satisfaction and contentment at some stage that becomes a real treasure.

- *Instead of running after mind's fabricated hungers, why not leave on HIM to regulate our appetites and provide accordingly.*

Clean hands

My hands were clean, when I came to this world,
I have done jobs, I may have to do, but let me be alert,
I don't know when I leave this world,
My hands may not have gathered some undesirable dirt.

When I have entered this world, I would naturally
do some deeds,
What sort of deeds, may not depend solely on my needs,
I would act according to the thoughts and controlling senses
I possess,
There is a criss-cross between thoughts and the controlling
senses, wins the one which is in excess.

When I am in the jungle of my thoughts, the controlling senses
are nowhere,
Shouldn't I search the controlling device in advance, lest I may
be swept somewhere,
I may be swayed somewhere, from where there is no return,
Dusty and dirty hands, bruised feelings and no chance
to take a turn.

The chances are great that I may not
remain in good taste,
I may develop an inward hate, the life may
look to be a waste,
I may still want to correct my unsteady gait,
It may not be too late to find a consoling gate.

Fix your mind on ME, be devoted to ME, worship ME and make obeisance to ME; thus linking yourself with ME and entirely depending on ME, you shall come to ME.

Srimad Bhagavadgita
Ch. 9

Law of love

Love is seated in one's head and heart,
The swing of life travels smoothly on its cart,
Love does not just begin at the time of one's birth,
It takes time for a being to understand its worth.

Some understand parent's love, some the love of wife,
And some do not understand it throughout the life,
Loving and understanding love are two different aspects,
Blind love, enveloped with lust, mostly ends with regrets.

Acceptance of love is to be returned with interest,
Whether it is mother, father, child or the rest,
Love investments never get lost or go waste,
Nature keeps its account, don't make decisions in a haste.

Human love can't be different from love of nature,
The nature loves not only humans but every creature,
The nature, unassuming keeps on fulfilling our every need,
But, does the nature does all this in some greed?

Greed and self-interest, no place in the loving path,
Understanding each others shortcomings in the life's cloth,
Accepting each other in the loving way,
Adjusting and understanding where my mistake lay.

- *Nature also wants love in return of love to its creatures.*

Forgiveness is within you

He has committed a big blunder,
He has spoiled our honour and image,
Don't leave him, he is not tender,
What he thought, he does not know my rage.

Life is to do all right deeds,
A gentleman always thinks the right way,
Did he do it intentionally?
He might be cursing that wrong day.

Everyone gets punishment for his mistakes,
Let the nature decide what action it takes,
When nature has its own way of punching,
Why the man takes unnecessary trouble of punishing?

What is required is to hold the stirring of the mind
and having a poise,
What is required is to hold the emotions,
What is required is to properly counsel him,
What is required is to lodge a complaint with HIM,
if necessary.

Quite possibly his mistake was only nature born,
Is it necessary then to blow the horn?
If he has done it intentionally,
Then none can save him naturally.

- *Think, small fights, at times, turn into big battles.*
- *We are only the appointed workers of the natural forces.*
- *Remember, HE is never a wrong-doer.*

Attachment

Is it possible to live without attachment ?
Can a man live with strict detachment ?
But this man may be called a cruel creature,
Would a man be liked less this particular feature ?

One is attached to his son,
The other to his sin,
Someone is attached to his cars,
Others to their buildings, jobs and bars.

Attachment is difficult to leave,
That mind is difficult to weave,
But, attachment may make a man sick,
At times, it becomes a poison to lick.

Is not there any medicine or trick ?
Towards happiness, isn't it a wall of cement and brick ?
It depends how much deeply one is attached,
It is the severity of this depth with which one is attacked.

Attachment is born in one's mind,
Then why is it so difficult to wind or unwind,
No doubt, mind is a difficult one to mind,
But, real love and attachment with God can make
worldly attachment less and lesser blind.

Attachment is the hunger of the mind. Let not this hunger become misery for you.

The man dwelling on sense-objects develops attachment for them; from attachment springs up desire, and from desire (unfulfilled) ensues anger.

Srimad Bhagavadgita
Ch. 2

Is it love or business

If I may get this job,
If I may clear this fog,
With HIM a treaty I make,
And wait for the cake.

I get what I wanted from HIM,
I celebrate my award,
I make him happy with the agreed reward,
I again make a fresh fruit getting treaty with HIM.

The life goes on and makes me busy,
Because of my treaties with HIM I get easy,
I continue to ask HIM every now and then,
And continue to offer HIM every then.

But, what HE requires, a treaty or love ?
Perhaps, constant love in return of constant love.

The devotees, however, who loving no one else constantly think of ME, and worship ME in a disinterested spirit, to those ever united in thought with ME, I bring full security and personally attend to their needs.

Srimad Bhagavadgita
Ch.9

Ignorance

Ignorance is the root cause of many evils,
It makes many men devils,
Blinded by ignorance, one's thinking remains closed in a nut,
A person may go astray without knowing his body hut.

Once a wrong notion sticks unaware and it is difficult to judge,
The life circles around, with no one to guide, that mind is difficult to budge,
What is the right path, it may become difficult to decide,
The ultimate way may be to engage a divine guide.

Ignorance clouds a life,
The life is shrouded in darkness,
The pity is, one does not feel ignorant,
Till someone opens the gates with mystical brightness.

Books can no doubt provide knowledge,
For erasing blind faiths, there is still a better college,
The awareness from within is the greatest source of wisdom,
The wise become the wiser, the wiser, more wiser as one walks in that within God's kingdom.

The omnipresent God does not receive the virtue or sin of anyone. Knowledge is enveloped in ignorance; hence it is that beings are constantly falling a prey to delusion.

In the case, however, of those whose said ignorance has been set aside by true knowledge of God, that wisdom shining like the sun reveals the supreme.

Srimad Bhagavadgita
Ch. 5

The portrait of a girl

A girl she bore,
Who can say she gets hate or adore,
A hidden silence falls on the house,
Arises against God a hidden feeling of grouse.

I longed for a son,
I don't know what ill we have done,
I wanted a heir,
Perhaps, God does not care.

A time later, the same girl develops a loving relation,
After all, it's a nature's well thought off creation,
In the mind of the minds, the son is still a glittering gold,
After all, who would look after when I am old ?

What haunts a man is his heir and old age,
He is a depressed being hiding something in his inner cage,
Why doesn't he rely on HIS design ?
Is a son all what is called divine ?

Is the daughter's birth a nature's crime ?
Or is it my mind's and my society's doctrine ?
A girl may be somewhat comparatively frail,
Given a chance she would not trail.

The girl has to leave her cage, to get into her husband's jail,
She enjoys the jail and starts a new love tale,
Parents lose what they earned and brought up in the past,
Daughter's smile doesn't make them feel that a paradise is lost.

She may be strong, mostly exists under others wilful might,
She may be bright, whether she has the right to her right,
All this, she has to maintain house's delight,
The weather may be rough, may be fine, she must continue
her flight.

The man is, at times, lost between love and duty,
Whether he should obey his mother or look to wife's beauty ?
The understanding is hard to achieve,
Whom and what he should leave ?

The life moves up and down,
Sometimes, the mother and somtimes the wife wears
the crown,
The whole life may not be spent in this struggle,
Thinking, weighing and understanding can solve this riddle.

A woman becomes enemy of another woman,
The man goes astray,
Unnecessary stress, unwanted teasing tension,
Is prudence not the only way ?

Why can't we change ?
Why can't we change our outlook ?
Why can't we change our hard attitudes ?
Why can't we change our social fabric ?

Everything changes,
The sun changes, the moon changes,
The earth changes, our body changes,
Why can't we change our social fabric ?

Why can't we equate the girl and the boy ?
Dowry, name, heirs, can't we put a why ?
Why can't the boy and girl bring equal amount of money ?
For enjoyment sake, both of them enjoy the honey.

It is only our thinking that makes a girl and her parents low,
When everyone knows that without her this world
can't grow,
A deeper insight can prove, that the boy's supremacy
is all hollow,
Our hard attitude makes this fact difficult to swallow.

A change in attitudes can bring heaven on earth,
When we can give a real meaning to girl's birth,
A time may come when we can turn towards her
a respectful eye,
And say to our hard attitudes hidden
within a wilful goodbye.

Who is stronger

Anyone, I can beat,
I have the greatest heat,
Everyone and anyone I can rule,
I can make anyone my tool.

My money is my might,
My position, I can move everything right,
I have the Himalayan height,
I am the brightest of the bright.

It is HIS, strength is not mine,
I am only drunk in my unreal strength's wine,
Stronger is the one who is wise,
My, My, My and I are all lies.

Strongest is the one, having all strengths, he is humble,
Hot, cold, sorrow or joy, he does not tremble.

Moonlit nights

Dear moon, why don't you glow in full every night?
Why don't you shower silver in full every night?
I long for your full appearance,
I dream about your full appearance.

I want to see you in full throughout,
Will you consider my demand, I doubt,
The moon says, I have my own limitations,
I can't vary the variations.

The sun lights the whole day very bright,
But, can't afford to light the night,
Says the moon, however, anything is bright,
Everything has a dark night.

Let us hope that the morning will be bright,
But, let us not forget, that there will again be night,
There is one thing that remains always bright,
The soul within doesn't see any night.

- *The nature teaches us that everything is not available in full and at all times.*
- *A thing which is available at all times, loses its value and importance.*
- *Others possessions may look big. They may have an invisible hollowness.*

The invisible mask

He used to wear artificial masks, he was tender,
The artificial one's got lost, as he grew with calendar,
Years had passed, I had completely forgotten,
When I felt he was again wearing something on his face.

It could not be seen, it had no colour,
It deceived, which he felt as valour,
He felt elated, it was all a dirty job of his mind,
Its short term advantages of name and fame had made
him blind.

When he deceived people, he would not call himself
a hypocrite,
He would consider himself a social player and consider himself
absolutely right,
He called them a hypocrite, they stretched their arm
in his direction,
Actually, all had lost one thing, i.e., the right direction.

Once a child's play has today become a selfish
game in reality,
One uses it often to settle old scores,
The actions are all automatic with a fixed mindset,
Who dare open one's mind's doors?

If one day he comes in contact with his soul,
He would understand the story as a whole,
His mind made him wear the mask,
And his mind alone can make him tear the mask.

- *Masks have the same colour, the depth of the masks are different.*
- *Let us think, what makes us wear the masks?*

Sans sympathy

Who cares for the others feelings,
Self-interest is the order of the dealings,
Have we become self-interest snatchers?
Sympathy is there, but remains only in wrappers.

Telling someone something in true and sincere sense,
May bring hate, scorn and a little remorse,
You may try to become honest,
Don't let everyone know, it may bring discomfort
in your nest.

Yours sincerely and yours faithfully are limited to only letters,
Otherwise, who identifies these letters,
Hatred is on the top of the list,
In fact for some, it becomes life's gist.

You want to enquire sincerely about someone's health,
Never be sure to get correct details, secrecy being the wealth,
You want to pay a goodwill visit or want to host,
Never be sure of others will, you may be meeting a ghost.

Thoughts and feelings make a man,
And thoughts and feelings make a demon,
At times, it may become difficult to understand a person, his
logic and action,
One may ponder, he belongs to which section.

Men possessing a demoniac disposition know not what is right activity and what is right abstinence from activity. Hence they possess neither purity (external or internal) nor good conduct nor even truthfulness.

Srimad Bhagavadgita
Ch.16

A mystic

I was with HIM, when I slept last night,
HE was with me, when I was up in the morning,
We meet every now and then,
HE gives me a treat every now & then.

I am bound with an invisible bind,
That sincere love and the relationship is of a different kind,
When my jobs get stuck up here and there,
HE comes for my help from somewhere.

My world without HIM is just dust,
In HIM, I put my absolute trust,
HE is the greatest friend I have ever met,
I feel very safe in HIS beautiful net.

He is the best tutor and guide,
Every step, I enjoy his ride,
HE is also a doctor to me,
His treatment is invisible and completely free.

What HE does for me I can't explain,
A sea of nice feelings which I retain,
HE is housed within me,
And as such everywhere with me.

- *Everyone is a prisoner, a prisoner of love, a prisoner of lust, a prisoner of pride, a prisoner of anger, a prisoner of prejudice and a prisoner of wealth and authority. Best be HIS prisoner.*

Spring

The flowers are blooming,
Beautiful leaves are growing,
Green, winds, all attract,
But to some eyes it has no effect.

It is not eyes, its mind's defect,
Beautiful designs of leaves and petals do not give any rest,
In the mind there is a different design,
There is no time to drink spring's wine.

Unlucky are those who can't observe nature's beauty,
Spring provides happiness amid duty,
If one is conscious of nature's beauty,
One can enjoy all the more his duty.

It is not spring for him who is worrying,
It is not spring for him who is sorrowing,
The spring is when you are cheerful,
The spring is when you are gleeful.

The spring comes only once a year,
The beautiful dresses trees and plants wear,
For you, spring can remain throughout the year,
If delightful and happy dresses you make your mind to wear.

- *Sorrows will hunt you till the end, until you learn to manage your emotions, through the vehicle of mind.*

What is past for me

For me past is not just past,
Let me learn and think of the future task,
Successes are dear to me as well as defeats,
I remember defeats told me, no retreats.

Hard times were there, difficult to manage,
Patience, however, held me without rage,
That patience was not in me in the earlier days,
Perhaps, that supreme power changed my ways.

Life as a whole has been a mixed experience,
There was always something with me that gave clearance,
Perhaps, because of HIS protection,
My past gives me a very soft reflection.

I have some messages to share,
Want to remain always happy, take care,
Sorrows will not leave you, they will stare,
Sorrows will hunt, be aware.

If possible within your mind, build two cages,
One for the sorrows and one for happiness,
They are partners since ages,
The mingling of the two makes sages.

The sage, whose mind remains unperturbed amid sorrows, whose thirst for pleasures has altogether disappeared, and who is free from passion, fear and anger, is called stable of mind.

Srimad Bhagavadgita
Ch. 2

The real pleasure : Dont's & Do's

Dont's ...
Don't be jealous of others
Don't get angered at others
Don't suffer from conceit
Don't misunderstand others
Don't criticise others unnecessarily
Don't hurt others
Don't be overambitious
Don't be in a hurry always
Don't be too much after materialistic comforts
Don't indulge in others affairs
Don't advise till asked for
Don't underestimate others and yourself
Don't get into sinful acts
Don't be misled by uneven flight of your mind

Do's ...
Be a positive thinker
Be patient
Be proactive
Always ready to help others
Have a feeling of love for all creatures in the world
Respect your equals and elders
Have a smiling face
Be a patient listener
Try to see things from others point of view
Be a hard worker
Always be ready to face criticism
Be logical
Take care of your physique and be alert
Have faith in God, meditate on HIM and be guided by HIM

The aging parents

Nearby, lived a friend of mine,
Many times, we sat, talked and dined,
With him, I felt very fine,
We talked from our own family to the divine.

I have seen his family, come up with two sons and no daughter,
One, he wanted to make an engineer and another a doctor,
His dream was fulfilled,
He was very thrilled.

He took many pains to bring them up,
Thinking always, when adults, the happiness
they would bring up,
The day came, they got the jobs,
He sat relaxed after clearing all fogs.

The days went off, the nights went off,
It appeared all his worries were off,
Now, was the time for them to marry,
Now, was the time for all to get merry.

The boys by then had different designs,
For them, getting married early, there were no signs,
They wanted to enjoy life,
For the time being without a wife.

The young want to live life in their own ways,
They do not want to remember their childhood days,
The parents want to see them grow in size,
Thinking, they have become wise.

Children are wise,
But, they want to dance, as their young mind flies,
One may thoughtfully fly,
Alongwith to satisfy the parents, why can't one try.

The boys had no time for all this to think,
More important was to dine and drink,
To help the parents, one may have a mindset,
Then, there is no problem to see them at rest.

These boys lacked this education,
In their mind, there was no such projection,
The parents hoped on,
And the time passed off.

One day, the younger one came up with a
proposal to marry,
He wanted to marry, one Cherry,
The father was happy to hear the news,
The son wanted to settle abroad, made the father sad
with his views.

The father had no way to stop the boy,
Now to make him happy or stop him, he had no toy,
The father had to agree,
And the son got ready to flee.

The girl was in a foreign country,
The boy married and settled there,
The parents sad and happy also, as their son had settled,
Prayed to God and wished good health here.

The young minds flew and had delight,
Enjoyed every day and night,
The parents who brought him up with great expectations,
Had nothing left with them, but broken hearts and dreams.

They consoled each other,
And had their eyes now fixed on the other.

The other one was very busy,
To make him agree to marry was not easy,
The parents used to think and think,
Many nights, they did not sleep a wink.

Do the parents not deserve any care?
Is it incorrect for parents to have any expectations?
Are the parents only for giving birth and
no expectations?
Should the parents detach themselves from children?

Was the action of the boy thoughtful and mature?
Why did he not think that parents are a part of his family?
Was it not proper on his part to discuss and consult?
Was something wrong with the parents or the boy?

Perhaps, he lacked in education,
What sort of education?
Perhaps, he could not control the flight of his mind,
His dreams were too strong before parent's dreams, which he
could not unwind.

One thing is clear, his parents he did severely hurt,
With his parents he was definitely curt,
And to add to that, he did not feel,
The wounds, only time would heal.

Following his brother, the other son also came up with a proposal,
He also wanted to settle abroad,
The parents looked at each other, confused,
All arguments got refused.

Finally, looking to their child's face, parents had to agree,
This child was also set free,
Before leaving, he met all near and dears,
For the parents, this was the beginning of tears.

The parents, frail and old,
In their house, that enthusiasm and everything had gone cold,
They always used to think, what was their mistake?
What action they did not take?

By now, all the tears had dried,
All the methods to control the mind they had tried,
They talked to themselves, we started alone,
We are once again all alone.

The departure of the sons, they could not bear,
They could not see anyone who was their near,
In this situation, I could give them one help,
I again advised them to take HIS help.

Perhaps, this was the time to meditate on HIM,
Perhaps, the God wanted them to be near to HIM,
Had they started, to be with HIM, in the earlier days,
They would have tackled such situations in
different ways.

The attachment towards the sons was too strong,
To be attached is not wrong,
Lesser the attachment,
Lesser the pain.

If you fix your thoughts on HIM,
Lodge your complaints with HIM,
HE would definitely get you solutions,
And in these situations, solutions come only from within.

Life is throughout a fight,
But, one wishes to have delight,
More difficult is the inner fight,
And the only way is to reach the inner light.

What mistake the children did?
To feel others sufferings, one has to remove the lust's lid,
For them, it was lust for materialistic world,
That made them deaf to their parent's word.

The old man could not bear the strain,
It was too much for his brain,
The old man ultimately died,
The lady who took so much pains for the family just cried.

The lady is today seen alone with her stick,
With her neighbours she is quite thick,
On her lips is God's name,
She does not care much for the outside game.

Everyone deserted her,
But, she found her way,
It looks she is always with HIM,
And HE is always with her.

She has always on her face, a brief smile,
It looks she is not sad for a while,
Her children come sometimes in years,
In those days, the great happiness she wears.

All the children love her,
She loves all the children,
One day when children go,
She stands happily to wish them good-bye.

She has gained the strength from within,
She has become wise from within.

Respect

Is the right to respect restricted only to a few?
Do all deserve respect, is a matter to review?
Only a few get respect, it is not new,
Some of the respected do not deserve respect is another view.

Why should everyone not get respect?
When everyone is HIS creation, then why disrespect?
How does anyone become high or low?
When everyone has to play his assigned role and then go.

I am the great officer of this place,
Whose place?
I am the owner of this building,
Whose building?

The God's places and buildings got him respect,
Without these assets, one gets disrespect,
At the hands of respected one's,
And will become respected one, getting God's assets once.

Giving respect to someone and disrespect to another,
Is one's mind's will,
But, when everyone is God's creation,
HE would not like disrespect to his own creation and will be against HIS will.

- *One does not become big by the riches alone, but also by the values of life he or she possesses, and commands respect accordingly.*
- *A man with stable mind would like to respect not only human beings, but all the creatures in the world.*

Sacrifice

One has to give something to get something valuable,
If not at that particular moment, then when you become able,
Without sacrificing there is no success,
As without pain there is no gain.

Do the sacrifices get lost?
Some or the other moment, they may give back their cost,
One has to spend something to get comfort,
One has to pay something to remove discomfort.

Sacrificing without a cause, with no return,
Is no easy task,
Even sacrificing for a known cause,
May, at times, become a difficult task.

Soldiers sacrifice their lives, they get medals and awards,
Hard work pays in terms of rewards,
When one is very young, parents sacrifice,
When parents in need, does not that demand sacrifice?

Sacrifice should be for a good cause,
Sacrifice should not be for an ill task,
Sacrifice should be for a sensible and good value,
Sacrifice may not bring ill for others and you.

Think carefully, an act which you may think as sacrifice,
May not be a sacrifice, and you may have to pay a heavy
price.

- *A few minutes of continuous sacrifice everyday in HIS meditation, may pay you heavy dividends.*
- *Sacrifices never get lost. Never shirk sacrifices.*

The love affair story

He met a girl,
She made the boy whirl,
He meets another girl,
Finds attraction in her curl.

He enjoys the company of both,
The love is on the path of growth,
They get alongwith their respective affairs,
Let someone or no one know about it,Who cares?

The boy meets everyday with one or another,
Sometimes, he likes the one and sometimes the other,
His mind, changing colour, keeps on,
The mind changes from one end to another every dawn.

He treats it as part of his life game,
Among friends he gets fame,
The so called love changes into lust,
They forget what is just.

The girls enjoy the trust,
Till the secret gets a bust,
Is it love or only a play?
The immature mind does not know where his or her mistake lay.

The emotions play high and low,
The boy does not know where to go,
Is there something lacking in the boy?
Or is there something lacking in his education?

Everyone wants to write his own love story,
Is it craze or carries some glory?
Unaware, the untidy mind gets into problems,
And then finds its solutions.

The boy at last decides on one,
And thinks the job is all done,
Unmindful, he does not care for the feelings of the other,
Does she have a heart of some other leather?

Was the beginning of the love tale thoughtful?
Can't a love tale be graceful?
Does love making not require any maturity?
Why we forget that something called dignity?

Who is responsible for all this ?
Shouldn't the boys and girls get educated?
Who is to blame?
The boy, the girl or the parents?

When everyone knows that there is a trap,
Then, where lies the gap?
After the selection of the girl,
The boy gets into another whirl.

The boy's parents do not accept the girl,
This starts up another quarrel,
The question hovers over, money, family and the caste,
The difference is very vast.

There is again shoot up of emotions,
On both sides, there is a mixture of allegations,
Fathers, mothers, all are confused,
The entry on either side is refused.

What will happen to the boy's and girl's mind?
Hot emotions turn everyone blind,
Once again the confusions arise,
From where these problems rise?

Who has gone wrong?
To whom the mistake belong?
The girl's side blame the boy,
The boy's side blame the girl.

The problem is difficult to solve,
The love is difficult to dissolve,
When you know, I know, it is happening everywhere,
Then, why the adults and the parents did not take care?

Either the boy's parents are wrong,
Their hard attitudes are too strong,
Or the boy and the girl are wrong,
But, their blind lust or love is too strong.

The two young minds are put to test,
Their education, career, all take rest,
Why not be proactive in approach?
Why not, in advance provide a coach?

The film story becomes the real education,
The rest all goes on vacation,
There is a difference between love and lust,
Everyone must understand what is just.

No doubt, love making is everyone's right,
How to control the flight of the kite?
How to control the flight of the mind?
And how to make the love lust less and lesser blind?

After long negotiations, the parents agree,
Make the boy and the girl free,
The boy and the girl think, their dream has come true,
The marriage comes through.

The girl's parents are happy,
The boy's parents are happy,
This marks the end of a tale,
But, this puts them on a real life testing trail.

Hours, days and months fly,
They feel everything else is a lie,
Gradually, the honeymooning comes to an end,
The life takes another bend.

The shortcomings of each other come to sight,
Naturally, they do not give delight,
Arises a tale of discussions,
They again try to find solutions.

The arguments turn into shouts,
They turn to even bouts,
The love story, which was till now a success,
Takes a turn around, each other, they assess.

Thinks the girl, she has landed in a trap,
Weeping, thinks of her mother's lap,
A confused state once again prevails,
The love story derails.

Did this story begin with love?
Or did it start with lust?
Real love ignores and accepts shortcomings,
Real love accepts a person in totality.

Marriage is such an institution,
Where there is, in fact, no place for resignation,
You can resign under the human law,
Remain united says, the natural law.

The love at first sight is not love, but lust,
If it is love, it should not rust,
We are all humans, we may have love at first sight,
A step taken once, with maturity, should not see left or right.

God has made this earth to make love,
Not a mockery of love,
He has installed a soul in every human being,
So that, respecting this soul, the God's part, everyone should respect and love every other being.

- *Deceiving in love may not be a crime in human's law, but is definitely a crime in nature's law.*
- *A crime is a crime, the punishment in some natural form is inevitable.*
- *Love situations are different from after marriage situations, which are difficult to envisage and hence the problems.*
- *A continued association automatically develops a sound, healthy and strong love.*
- *What matters in love relationships?*
  Is it love, company, nearness?
  Is it money, appearance, selflessness?
  Is it trust, nature, togetherness?
  or
  Is it the understanding that matters?
  It is the understanding that really matters.

Kite flying

Thinking higher in the skies, feet on earth,
Let me survey, if I am that worth,
I think of playing such a game,
Which does not really fit in my frame.

Thinking high is a good trait,
If I have the art of weighing the weight,
I plan for something in life, which I am not sure,
Illogically planned or desired may not give you a difficult sore.

An unfulfilled desire can give such a sore,
Later on, you may think, that idea, why I bore?
The desires spring up day and night,
The art lies in measuring their height.

Let me loosen the strings of my kite,
Will I not mind, when my kite gets a bite?
Flying the kite to the desired height is my right,
Its downfall will undoubtedly not give delight.

Let my measured and weighed desires fly,
Let my desires not die,
God's will will come on the way,
Let me wait for the proper time and day.

- *A realistic assessment and approach in life always helps.*
- *Learn to live happily alongwith an unfulfilled desire.*

Cricketing

Everyone is a cricketer,
Everyone is cricketing,
The ball that falls on us are our problems,
The punch we make are the solutions.

As the type of the ball, the problems keep on changing,
Sometimes serious and sometimes hurting, the problems keep on raining,
The batsman cannot sit at calm,
A heavy bowling may do some harm.

Here the bowling can come from any direction,
You can't raise any objection,
Hitting the problems, many times you are caught,
Here you bring in solutions from what you were taught.

You have all opponents around,
You are just all alone in the ground,
You do not know, from which direction, the problem falls,
You keep on getting calls.

You may be alert, there is a possibility of
getting caught and getting bowled,
The opponents are ready with their sleeves rolled,
You may make centuries,
One day you are definitely going to be bowled.

Your teammates cannot help you in case of need,
They will say, you had to be out, you did not properly read,
Stress of life makes you exhausted,
You are finally rejected.

There is no one around you,
Don't forget your friend within.

The show off business

Today is the first day of the year,
Only one thing we hear,
Wish you a happy new year,
A very very happy new year.

But, when people see anyone grow,
They have a different situation on their brow,
Does anyone want to see, in reality, anyone happy?
Or is it a hoax?

Everyone is not like this,
Some peoples' wish is really a wish,
One has to cleanse one's mind,
One has to make efforts to become of that kind.

To make everyone happy, every year comes one day,
And this is everyone's birthday,
People connect and say, happy birthday,
Many, many happy returns of the day.

The other day, the same man, with his feelings they play,
Thinks the man, they were fine with me, the earlier day,
To keep relations, one has to wish,
At the heart, one may have a hot, sour, bitter or a sweet dish.

The smile is another deceiver,
Many times, fails to understand the receiver,
The next hour, the same one is banged,
A little less than to be hanged.

This smile is only a style,
It does not take even a while,
My feelings, why should anyone know,
To hell, let them go.

People make many goodwill phones,
But, at times, to know what is happening at the other end,
After the phone, they will talk, laugh and ridicule,
Why, this is the latest trend.

One has to look sincere,
The mind, any colour, let it wear,
My mind, it should remain at rest,
Others, let it go bust.

At the party and get-togethers, beautiful dresses
everyone wears,
Talks, laughs, hi and bye everyone hears,
At the back, begin the talks,
See how he walks.

This one has gone old,
When he was gold,
He was always like this,
When was he wise.

And what he is doing,
He is so boring,
Soon, they come across,
At once, they say, hello boss.

What saree she is wearing ?
Looks to be an ordinary one,
Not that ordinary,
She can't have a big one.

You see the make up she is having,
She can't do better than this,
What she thinks of herself ?
A little later, they meet with a kiss.

The life goes on like this,
No one cares, her or his,
In this life, is the mind at rest?
I think, the mind is always put to test.

Does not simplicity in life pay ?
Why, all this play ?
Perhaps, to show one is superior,
And the other is inferior.

Is he superior, who wears the crown ?
One has to prove by his or her actions, that he or
she wears a crown,
Today, no one is spared, whether with crown,
Or a little down.

All this show, comes the death of someone,
The news reaches everyone,
You must go to his cremation, dear,
But, he misbehaved and did not speak to me during
the last one year.

Whatever, past is past, forget everything,
You go, leave everything,
In life, you could not be good friends,
After death, be friends.

Everyone is not like this,
One may want to show, what he is,
But, by his this action,
He may not get a good public reaction.

Should not man to man relations be simple and clean?
Then, why so complex?
Let us ponder,
And let us make relations less and lesser complex.

The making of a human being

Everyone wishes his son or daughter,
To become an engineer or doctor,
This is all clear,
Whether their aim includes their kids to become a good human being, for the life they have to steer ?

The child gets love from all the directions,
His behaviour from time to time needs corrections,
He may not become a stubborn child,
And many, like this go wild.

If the parents themselves do not have the right thinking,
The child will grow just winking,
And, then they say, where the child has gone,
And, then arises the question, why he went wrong?

The parents have first to become good human beings,
Then they can make their children good beings,
Children observe right from the beginning what their parents do,
The children do not hesitate to do what their parents do.

Good values make good human beings,
Not only by knowing, but by thoughts and deeds,
Knowing something is like any other subject,
The test is when and how a testing situation one meets.

You may have many friends,
But, are they your real friends?
Only time will show if the friendship is true,
Still a lot and lot depends upon you.

It is difficult to get true friends today,
May be because that softness is now not our way,
Our attachment towards other things,
Has made us detached from other beings.

Man has reached the moon not neighbours,
In relationship also we have become traders,
We trade over the gifts,
If not properly dealt, creates rifts.

Rifts suddenly become serious,
Dejected, they leave us,
When self-interest is on the path,
It can't be covered with any cloth.

Self-interest shows its effect one day,
It is hidden deep inside our clay,
Can't be cut by any ray,
Finally, it changes our way.

It makes selfish friends,
Not true friends,
It may satisfy one's greed,
But, he may not be your friend in need.

Sincerity in friendship is a must,
Let us not be swayed by lust,
It is important to be sincere towards man,
As is to be sincere towards God.

If one does not know, how to adjust with others,
How to cooperate with others,
Then, how can they be true to others,
How can they bring love and peace for others.

Honesty is a good trait,
Let us not make its trade,
Honesty has its place in all steps of life,
Honesty plays its role even in strife.

The earth stands because of its honesty,
If the sun and moon become dishonest,
Nothing will remain here,
Even the animals will die who are not dishonest.

Why a man is dishonest ?
It is because of the thinking faculty that God has provided,
Misusing the good brain provided,
Between honest and dishonest, the humans stand divided.

Speaking a lie,
Why feel shy?
Speaking the truth, I may have to cry,
Speaking a lie, an easier way, why not try?

One tries the easier way,
It becomes a habit one day,
Humans should discourage speaking lie,
If they do not want truth to die.

Speaking the truth requires courage,
One may have to face one's rage,
If we are true and honest to our actions,
Why, then the fear of the reactions?

Real boldness in a person comes from honesty,
An inner cowardice develops from dishonesty,
Bold are those who do the things the right way,
They accept where their mistake lay.

Defending oneself boldly is another good trait,
Honesty is the best force behind this trait,
Honesty is the pillar upon which anything can rest,
Honesty takes us to the crest.

Deceiving with boldness is in fashion,
It does not see man to man relation,
It forgets that everyone is God's creation,
And is only one's mind's creation.

Deceiving springs up from hunger for different things,
This hunger springs up in one's mind,
No doubt, mind is a difficult thing to catch,
But, love and kindness also spring up in the mind.

Cruelty and kindness both crop up in the mind,
It is a question of bending the mind,
It is a question of training the mind,
Depends upon you which way you wind.

Cruelty and bravery may not be mixed,
Brave is ready to face pain and suffering,
Cruel has the desire to cause pain and suffering,
The roles of the two are different and fixed.

One can be cruelly deceived,
But, can't be bravely deceived,
A brave can also be kind,
A brave can have a stable and tidy mind.

Kind man should not be considered weak,
When attacked he may know how to treat,
A man may be meek,
But, he may have the strength and courage for difficult
situations, to meet.

A brave is far from fears,
He should have no place for tears,
In the life's battle field or war field,
He is not expected to yield.

A brave may have firm faith in God,
He may surrender to the Lord,
He may be with HIM,
And become strong within.

A person with a strong mind power,
A person with strong will power,
His strong will can take him to places,
And can defeat all in races.

By serving the people, he may think he is serving the God,
No one dare put in his right path, any rod,
God would guide him in his own way,
So that he does not become cruel in any way.

He should have his anger under control,
He should have his emotions under control,
Let any problems and difficulties role,
He should not lose sight of his goal.

He should have respect for others,
He should have love for others,
He may not unnecessarily hurt anyone,
He may not unnecessarily cause sufferings for anyone.

He may avoid fault-finding,
Even if he has to indulge in criticism,
He may speak and mend his words in such a way,
That the criticism may not appear as criticism.

A brave may know how to deal with life's stress,
Leaving everything on HIM, he should enjoy even small recess,
He should know how to assess,
And how to have access.

He should not burn his heart in jealousy,
He should have a proper feel of the reality,
Far away from illusions,
He should believe more in resolutions.

Happiness should not be far away from him,
If he keeps himself near HIM,
Real happiness arises from contentment,
Real happiness arises from some detachment.

Strong desires to possess something (worldly objects),
Which is beyond your reach,
May give you unhappiness,
Which only time will teach.

If want to possess something beyond reach,
May request God, as everything is within HIS reach,
But, here also, you may be put to a severe test,
Only then, you may reach the crest.

You may find happiness in small things,
If you get carried away in His wings,
Too many unfulfilled desires may give you unrest,
But, once you reach satisfaction, you will be at rest.

The strength lies in having patience,
A brave man without patience,
Is like an iron wire, which breaks on twisting,
One of the worst enemies of a man is impatience.

Patience is a weapon of the wise,
It is a must if one wants to rise,
Patience needs practice to reach,
Only your mind can help you to teach.

Tolerance tests the brave,
The situation may be grave,
The brave remains cool,
The opponent may use any tool.

The strong need not be impolite,
He should make the weak feel light,
Speech can win over anyone,
Appropriate words can help win weak over the strong one.

Rudeness gathers force from the pride,
One cannot go smoothly for long taking its ride,
Softness can bring in delight,
To remain happy is everyone's right.

Soft words do not cost anything,
Think of the happiness they bring,
Some people are averse to others happiness,
Want to capture happiness at the cost of others happiness.

Some use strength to make others unhappy,
Some use power to make others unhappy,
This cannot be the job of a brave man,
This can be the job of a selfish and coward man.

The brave is the one who does not worry about it,
He gets a way to face it,
He finds a way to defeat it,
With God, the happiness, he gets it.

Getting happiness at others cost is not real happiness,
Snatching happiness from others is not real happiness,
Real happiness is the one that is provided by nature,
Real happiness is the one which one gets taking care
of every creature.

The strong one cannot command real happiness,
The brave one cannot command that happiness,
Till they get the happiness from within,
Till they beat the sorrow within.

A brave may or may not be physically strong,
He must be strong within,
At times, the strength within overpowers the strength outside,
Because endurance is a power within.

Distributing happiness should be the aim,
Providing peace should be everyone's aim,
Remaining in peace should be everyone's aim,
Helping others to get peace should be everyone's aim.

Wearing a smiling face,
Regardless of caste and creed, everyone, one should embrace,
A human being should treat everyone as a human being,
And no other different being.

Amid everything we should not forget grace,
Let it be any race,
You win or anyone else wins,
It is ultimately the God's win.

As the God lives in every human being,
To get respect is the right of every being,
To get happiness is the right of every being,
To get love is the right of every being.

All these qualities and many other may be
inaccessible in an ordinary way,
Ours is a body made of clay,
To infuse the best qualities into this clay,
We may have to search, the maker, where HE lay.

- *Absolute fearlessness, perfect purity of mind, constant fixity in the Yoga of meditation for the sake of Self-realization, and even so charity in its Sattvika form, control of the senses, worship of God and other deities as well as of one's elders including the performance of Agnihotra (pouring oblations into the sacred fire) and other sacred duties, study and teaching of the Vedas and other sacred books as well as the chanting of God's names and praises, suffering hardships for the discharge of one's sacred obligations and straightness of mind as well as of the body and senses;*
- *Non-violence in thought, word and deed, truthfulness and geniality of speech, absence of anger even on provocation, disclaiming doership in respect of actions, quietude or composure of mind, abstaining from malicious gossip, compassion towards all creatures, absence of attachment to the objects of senses even during their contact with the senses, mildness, a sense of shame in transgressing against the scriptures or usage, and abstaining from frivolous pursuits;*
- *Sublimity, forbearance, fortitude, external purity, bearing enmity to none and absence of self-esteem—these are the marks of him, who is born with the divine gifts, Arjuna.*
- *Hypocrisy, arrogance and pride, and anger, sternness and ignorance too—these are the marks of him, who is born with demoniac properties.*

Srimad Bhagavadgita
Ch. 16